WHY I AM STILL A CATHOLIC

A CATHOLIC

VOLUME SIX

The Music of My Faith

by
Steve Gignac

WHY I AM STILL A CATHOLIC
Volume Five
THE MUSIC OF MY FAITH
by STEVE GIGNAC

© 2017 by Steve Gignac

Edited by Dr. Ronda Chervin
Designed by James Kent Ridley
Published by Goodbooks Media
Printed in the U.S.A.

ISBN-13: 978-1546431022
ISBN-10: 1546431020

Steve Gignac is a retired printer who has dedicated his anointed musical talents to furthering the flourishing charismatic prayer ministry he shares with his wife, Carol.

GOODBOOKS MEDIA
3453 Aransas Street
Corpus Christi, Texas, 78411
goodbooksmedia.com

ABOUT THE
WHY I AM STILL A CATHOLIC
SERIES OF BOOKLETS

by Ronda Chervin, Ph.D., Editor

Dr. Ronda is a Professor of Philosophy, a Presenter on Catholic TV and Radio, and a Dedicated Widow

In the year 2016 I read somewhere that 60% of Catholics have left the Church or only attend occasionally!

I was shocked! Myself a convert from an atheist but Jewish background, Jesus, manifested and coming to me, in the Catholic Church is the greatest joy in my life…from time into eternity!

How could it be that so many Catholics have lost faith in a church that offers so much?

I believe it was the Holy Spirit that suggested to me a remedy.

Suppose the parish racks had little booklets written by strong believers, such as myself, describing why we are still Catholics in spite of many of the same experiences which have alienated other Catholics! Such a series of booklets could attract wavering Catholics or be given by strong Catholics to family and friends who have left us. In this way our series was born.

So, now I address all wavering Catholics, and all those who have left the Catholic faith, and beg you to give us one more chance. Could it hurt to say a little prayer, such as this?

Jesus, if you are really the Son of God, and you want me to receive fullness of grace through the Word and Sacraments in the Catholic Church, open me to the witness of the writers of these booklets. As they tell me why they are still Catholics, please tell me why I should still be a Catholic!

"The Church is like a great ship being pounded by the waves of life's different stresses. Our duty is not to abandon ship, but to keep her on her course."
St. Boniface

Saint Cecilia, Patroness of Musicians, pray for us.

I was born and grew up in East Hartford, Connecticut. My father was in the military and my mother worked as a professional secretary. I have one brother and two sisters. We lived in Mayberry Village. As a young boy, I received the sacraments in the Catholic Church. Four of us would go as a family to church every Sunday. My younger brother and sister were born years later. As I got older, church was no longer a family priority. My Dad worked many hours and my Mom tried to keep the home running smoothly while holding down a full-time job.

I was very shy and timid as a child and young teen. I became a loner in junior high and in high school. I took in a lot and was sensitive and caring.

In junior high school, my best friend Jeff moved in next door. Jeff's father played guitar and taught him how to play. Jeff and I became good friends and did everything together. He taught me how to play guitar and we enjoyed playing together after school. He taught me basic chords and simple songs that he learned. I didn't have a lot friends; Jeff was and still is a blessing in my life. I found out the story about his father many years after he moved away.

It was a day like any other; Jeff and his brother kissed their Mom and Dad goodbye and left for

school. When they came home that afternoon, they found out that Dad had packed up and left the family. The only thing he didn't take with him was his guitar. Jeff picked up his Dad's guitar and played and played, sometimes for six hours at a time as a way of grieving the loss of his father.

When it came time to

upgrade his guitar, Jeff sold his father's guitar to me. This was my very first guitar. What a gift! I was about fifteen at the time. I felt it was anointed with a spiritual comfort that God gave to me.

The sacraments have had a positive influence in my life. They have helped me appreciate the gift of worship music and have strengthened my faith as a Catholic.

Sing the words and tunes of the psalms and hymns when you are together, and go on singing and chanting to the Lord in your hearts.

Ephesians 5: 19

BENEFIT DINNER

I was honored one day by a call from a friend at a parish where I played music at a First Friday Healing Mass every month. The parish was planning a benefit dinner for Kristina and her family. Kristina's twin sister died in a tragic car crash.

As I was leaving my home, I felt a nudge to take my guitar. I never do things like that for a non-music affair. If there was an opening to play, I would walk through that door. If not, it was no big deal.

My wife and I arrived at the dinner and rekindled old friendships. It was a beautiful affair that we very much enjoyed. Toward the end of the night, I spoke with John who emceed the event. I said to him that I had my guitar and was prepared to play a song for Kristina and her mother.

John said to me: "Oh Steve, I wish you said something earlier." Since people were leaving, I said: "Maybe a smaller crowd is better than a larger crowd." John said I could do what I wanted and pointed to the microphone.

Before playing, I asked Kristina and her mother if I could play a song for them. They said it would be very lovely. Just before I set the guitar up and started playing, I looked over the room and saw an amazing sight.

People were getting up to leave and saying their goodbyes. Men were breaking down tables to put them away. People were in and out of the kitchen, bringing in left-over food to be put away. It was this menagerie of busy people going in every direction.

I felt: "It's now or never." So I announced that I would sing a song for Kristina and her mother. As I started to play, there was a supernatural hush that came over the room. Everyone stopped to listen. It was amazing. Kristina and her mother were deeply moved. I was too.

ing to Him, play to Him. Tell of all His marvels!

Psalm 105:2

MY FRIEND JOE

he gift of music has been good to me. So many doors have opened when I said yes to playing music and singing for God and His Glory.

My friend Joe is a man of great suffering and was facing a major change in his life. Because of medical complications, he was facing having one of his legs cut off above the knee. That was his only option.

It was very stressful and I was praying for him. One day, I felt that God wanted me to take my guitar to the hospital and play music for him the day before his operation. As we were driving on the highway, the wind was blowing some tall trees on both sides of us. They were bowing as if to let me know that I made a good decision.

When we arrived at his hospital room, his eyes got big when we entered the room and he saw my guitar. I said: "Joe, I want to play a few songs to comfort you in this time of struggle and pain." So I took my guitar out and played and played. As I did, I saw Joe singing away with me.

It seemed that the music took him to another place for a while. I chose the song: "Be Not Afraid." As I played, Joe welled up and sang along with me. By the end of the song, streams of tears were flowing from his eyes. He thanked me for coming and told me he was at the end of his strength: emotionally, spiritually and physically. Through music, God gave him peace, calm and strength.

The next day, the operation went very well. Joe was in great spirits after the ordeal and both of us learned what friendships can do when guided by the Holy Spirit.

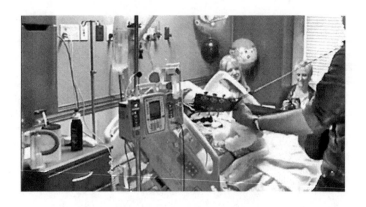

MUSIC FOR NORMAN

 took my guitar to a rehab place where a dear friend was recovering from heart problems. He had just turned 90 years old the day before.

Six of us went to visit him to find out how he was doing. We walked into his room that he shared with another patient who, at the time, was taking a nap. I said that I had come to play a few songs for him. His wife took us to an empty sitting room. I took out my guitar and started playing: *Amazing Grace.* As I looked, I saw him singing away. His face beamed with delight.

Pretty soon, people came down the hall because they heard the music and all of us singing. One lady came to the doorway in her wheelchair. My wife waved for her to come in. She wheeled herself up near to me. When I played *How Great Thou Art*, she welled up with tears. As we sang, streams of tears rolled down her face. She never missed a note or a word. When I finished, there was a sacred hush for about a minute. I thanked God for calling me there and blessing all of us in those moments.

STEVE'S GUITAR

 One day, my wife and I were getting ready to go to a Marian Day of Reflection at a place called "My Father's House." Father Bill started the retreat center decades ago. As I was leaving home, I got a nudge to bring my guitar. I put it in the back of my van and drove to Moodus, CT. Father Bill had no idea my wife and I were coming.

As we pulled into the parking lot, the first person we saw was Father Bill. Before we could say hello, he looked over at us and yelled across the yard: "Did Steve bring his guitar?" We were both delighted and amazed. I ended up playing music for the day of reflection and the Mass. God is so good!

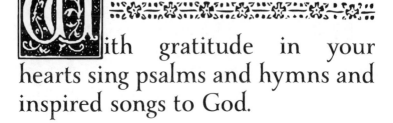

With gratitude in your hearts sing psalms and hymns and inspired songs to God.

Colossians 3:16

FAREWELL ISABELLA

One **December day**, I received some tragic news about a good friend of mine. Her 19-year-old daughter had died in a tragic car crash. My friend and her husband were devastated. I prayed: "God, what are you doing?"

Several days later, I got a call from my friend's mother. She asked me to play music with our mutual friends, Ed and Donna, at her granddaughter's funeral Mass. I responded: "Yes, it would be a great honor." Due to busy schedules, we could not practice together until the morning of Isabella's funeral. We depended totally on the Holy Spirit to bring things together.

I had taken my public address system with me just in case it was needed. Some churches have state of the art audio equipment while others have next to nothing. I wanted to get a good sound check before the Mass started.

To my frustration, I could not obtain a key to unlock the choir loft. The maintenance man, who had the only key, was on a coffee break. He only returned 45 minutes before Mass started. In the choir loft, he showed me where to plug into the house system. When I asked where the controls are located for the sound system, he said: "They are under lock and key and no one touches them." That's because a professional sound company set the volumes of all the microphones and instrument jacks. So much for bringing my own sound system!

We only had a half-hour to practice our songs together. Talk about a lesson in trust! In the choir loft, we prayed together and took some deep breaths. We could not hear ourselves singing because there were no monitor speakers. In our prayers we said to God: "It's all yours Lord. Use us as you will for your glory."

My heart was deeply touched as the church filled with people, standing room only. I estimated there were about one thousand people in the church. It is the biggest crowd where I have ever played. Nearly three quarters of the people were teenagers and young adults from the same high school where Isabella had graduated only one year before. We were amazed and blessed beyond anything we could have asked for or imagined.

THE LITTLE ONES

ith my friends Jim and Ed and my brother Peter, four of us played music and sang in harmony at three weekend Masses. We played for the Saturday evening Vigil Mass at Saint Christopher Church; the 11 am Sunday Mass at Saint Mary Church; and the 5:30 pm Mass at Saint Isaac Jogues Church on Sunday evening. It was a busy and rewarding schedule for us, to say the least.

When we played at Saint Mary Church in the morning, there was a little girl and her mother who would come to us after Mass; say hello and thank us for the music. The little girl was very pretty but also very shy. She used to look at me with big wonder-filled eyes and just gaze at me. I thought she was mesmerized by the music but later found out she was captivated by me. She was only 4 or 5 years old.

Each week, the little girl and her mother would greet us. One day, her mother said to her: "Go and give Mr. Gignac a big hug." She did so and ran back to her mother. Week after week, she came up to me with a hug. She became very comfortable with me; and I always made her feel very special.

One day after Mass, she came running down the aisle without her mother this time. She jumped into my arms and nestled her head against my chest. I was humbled and said: "My Lord, who am I that you would send this precious little one to me?"

GOD'S STANDING OVATION

ne of my favorite memories is when my wife worked as a Director of Religious Education in our parish. She had asked me to play music for the second-grade children's First Reconciliation service. I had come early to set up music equipment for their practice session. As I sang and practiced in the empty church, I heard the side door open. Our pastor entered and nodded hello to me. Then he walked up and down the aisles as he prayed the rosary while I praised God in song. It was a sacred time; and I felt that we were one in setting the spiritual stage for the children.

My wife led the young students into the church for practice, so they would be comfortable making their First Confession the following week. I was playing the guitar and singing as she led them into their pews. I noticed that one young boy could not take his eyes off me as he walked in the line. He was amazed. I thought that he might never have heard live music in a church. He turned his head and continued to gaze at me even as he sat down in the pew. I had a sense of awe in the way the Holy Spirit had touched him deeply. When I finished singing, he jumped to his feet and gave me the greatest standing ovation. He alone clapped for me, that is until he realized he was the only one doing so. Then he sheepishly sat down. I chuckled to myself and said: Thank you Lord for your standing ovation from this precious little boy."

MYSTERY GUEST

I **was playing music** for a healing Mass at Saint Thomas Seminary one evening. As I was setting up, I noticed a man walking down the side aisle of the empty church. He came up to me on the altar and asked: "Are you the musician for tonight?" I said: "Yes I am." He said: "That's great." I noticed that he was carrying a small case; and I asked: "What is in your case?" He told me it was his violin. I asked if he was a musician and he said "Yes." I asked how long he had been playing the violin; and he responded: "Fifty-one years!" Then the thought came to me that I should ask him to play music with me. I really didn't know him. I had never seen him before. That still small voice inside kept saying: "Ask him to play." So I asked him: "Would you like to play music with me at the Mass?" He responded: "What are you doing for songs." I showed him the list and said : "Here they are." He said he knew some but not all. If he could stand so that he could see me playing my guitar, he would follow me. I didn't know what to expect. I had never heard him play; and there was no time to go over the songs. I was totally trusting in God to work this out.

Nothing could have prepared me for what I was about to hear. It was the most amazing violin playing I have ever heard. He was playing octaves and doubling up on the strings. It was like something out the heavenly choir. It greatly enhanced the worship at Mass. What a unique gift he shared with me and all present. After the Mass, he came up to me and shook my hand. He said: "It was so great to play with such an accomplished musician as yourself. I was greatly humbled by my special guest.

MERCY FOR ALEX

hen I play my music, it brings comfort to others as well as myself. I didn't realize how much comfort it brings until a terrible tragedy happened a few years ago that made me appreciate, even more, my gift of music.

I was watching the news one evening and heard that some friends of ours who lived close to us had the worst thing happen to them. It was reported that a young husband and wife, who had three small children, had been found dead at their home. It was an incomprehensible blow to their parents, families, friends and the closely-knit community in which we live. Their two deaths were a priority profile case in the media. We were "blown away" by the series of events that led to their two deaths.

My wife and I went to the dead husband's family home to be with his parents and give our condolences in person. I took my guitar with me. We arrived at the home and knocked on the front door. We knew it had been an agonizingly long day for them. So we decided to stay only ten or fifteen minutes. I left my guitar in my van. We went in and hugged and talked for awhile. Up until the time we arrived, there was family coming in and out of the house all day. They had newspaper reporters, many telephone calls and no time for rest.

I believe with my whole heart that God opened up a period of time just for the four of us. My wife said I had my guitar and would play a few songs if they wished. Both of them immediately said yes. So I brought my guitar inside. We prayed the Sorrowful Mysteries of the Rosary together. Then I played and played and played for them. Some songs we sang together. Other songs were accompanied by their mourn-filled weeping. We sang together, cried together and prayed together for two-and-a-half hours. There was not one single telephone call or knock on the door that evening. Isn't God so good that He mourns and suffers with us? We left that evening feeling empowered by the Holy Spirit of consolation for our dear friends burdened with inexplicable grief.

LAURA'S SONG

I love to play my guitar for God. My first stepping out came many years ago when a good friend of mine was having her marriage blessed in the church. She asked me to play a song at her marriage ceremony, but only if I wanted to do so. She did not want me to feel pressured. So I decided to play one song.

I was used to playing with my music group; and so it was the very first time I played alone in public. It was an amazing experience. I felt nervous but empowered at the same time. It was the beginning of something really grand.

In the morning, I played a song at my friend's wedding. After the Mass, my girlfriend and I stopped by the wedding reception on our way home. While playing my song at the wedding reception, I was sweating intensely; and I felt power go out of me. I was light-headed after singing with all my might — for the very first time alone in public.

In the same evening, I played music at a monthly Healing Mass with my music group. When I got home at the end of a day with double music blessings, I was touched this all happened on the day of my birth.

God is so amazing and good! My friend told me that I was videotaped while singing my song. She commented that she and her husband watched it time and again. She felt honored to be my friend. To this day, she is still dear to my heart as a friend.

e has put a new song in my mouth, a song of praise to our God.

Psalm 40:3

FORGIVENESS

I've had many jobs over the years. One of them was a retreat center where I enjoyed working. I was a cook and maintenance man. This place was very sacred and peace-filled. I used to take my guitar to the Chapel and play every song I knew before the Blessed Sacrament. Sometimes, hours and hours seemed like minutes. I was living on the premises. It was a three-story building with over a hundred rooms for retreatants. It was very sacred, quiet and a real balm for my soul. Many, many great memories followed.

Another dear memory I had was playing my guitar at a special Mass where a famous priest and author presided and gave a special teaching. When it came time for Holy Communion, I felt unprepared to receive the Host. As Father drew new to me, I said to him: "I am sorry Father; but I am not prepared to receive the Body and Blood of Christ. He turned and walked back to the altar where he set the chalice down. He came back and gave me absolution for my sins right there on the altar. Then he went back to get the chalice and distributed Holy Communion. I was so empowered by the Holy Spirit that I felt as if I had sung with the voices of a hundred men.

I will sing a new song to You, O God; upon a ten-string lyre I will sing praises to You,

Psalm 144:9

CONCERT FOR JUDY

A **number of years ago**, my wife's best friend died of ovarian cancer. She was moved to a hospice near the shore for her remaining days on earth. She always loved my music. I took my guitar and my wife and I headed down to see her. It was about an hour journey by car.

When we arrived, we went to her room that she shared with three other women. We visited for awhile. With the permission of her roommates, I took my guitar out and played songs for her.

To my delight and surprise, a woman who was the music therapist happened to walk by and heard my music. Unbeknown to me, she entered the room and listened for a while. Then she came forward to introduce herself. She said my music was beautiful and asked if she could get her guitar to play some songs. We said yes; that would be lovely. So she got her guitar and came back to play a few songs. It was a tender and beautiful moment that we all treasured.

She then asked me if there were songs we could

play together. We did so and gave our dear friend Judy an amazing memorable private last concert on her deathbed. We played together as if we had practiced for years.

This all happened in the morning. About noon, my wife and I decided to take a break for lunch and let our friend rest while we were out of the room. When we came back from lunch, we found out from the nurses that we could wheel our friend's bed down the hall to a beautiful large patio overlooking the water. It was a bright and warm day. Our friend had always loved being by the water. I took out my guitar and played almost every song I knew. By the look on her face, our friend was almost in heaven; and so were we.

We then wheeled her back to her room that evening and thanked God for loving us so tenderly.

Our friend died a few days later; but I will always treasure the last moments we spent with her when she was alive.

In conclusion, I have had many music experiences over the years. It has continued to bless my life. I hope these stories bless you in a special way as well.

Carol and Steve

ost Merciful Jesus, Goodness Itself, You do not refuse light to those who seek it of You. Receive into the abode of Your Most Compassionate Heart the souls of those who have separated themselves from Your Church. Draw them by Your light into the unity of the Church, and do not let them escape from the abode of Your Most Compassionate Heart; but bring it about that they, too, come to glorify the generosity of Your mercy.

St, Faustina, *Diary*, 1219

To get a little sense of Steve's music go to WCATradio.com and click on Programs, then on Fridays, *Why I am Still a Catholic* and then click on the blue link and scroll to Friday, March 17, 2017 for the show with Steve's wife, Carol, and Steve talking about his music among other topics.

Bulk purchases of booklets in this series can be arranged by contacting fauxpas@swbell.net.

All the titles published to date can be viewed online at
http://goodbooksmedia.com/still-catholic.html

50350528R00024

Made in the USA
Middletown, DE
29 October 2017